Ashes

Prose Play

Kenneth Weene and Umar O. Abdul

Edited by Tendai Rinos Mwanaka

Cover art: Let The Dead Bury The Dead © Tendai Mwanaka

Mwanaka Media and Publishing Pvt Ltd,
Chitungwiza Zimbabwe

*

Creativity, Wisdom and Beauty

1

Publisher: Tendai R Mwanaka

Mwanaka Media and Publishing Pvt Ltd *(Mmap)*

24 Svosve Road, Zengeza 1

Chitungwiza Zimbabwe

mwanaka@yahoo.com

www.africanbookscollective.com/publishers/mwanaka-media-and-publishing

https://facebook.com/MwanakaMediaAndPublishing/

Distributed in and outside N. America by African Books Collective

orders@africanbookscollective.com

www.africanbookscollective.com

ISBN:978-1-77906-486-8

EAN:9781779064868

DISCLAIMER

All views expressed in this publication are those of the author and do not necessarily reflect the views of *Mmap*.

3

Characters

- WYNDEL BLACKMAN: A black American in his earl thirties
- MOMMA: Wyndel's mother
- CUSTOM AGENT: Custom officer at the air port
- SEGUN: A taxi driver, a Yoruba man from Lagos
- AKIN: Segun's son, a graduate of Theatre Arts
- UFEDO: A pretty young Igala lady, educated, soon to become ATA IGALA's third wife
- ATA: The ATA (King) of Igala Kigndom
- ACHIMI: King's jester
- OHIOGA: The palace chief priest of *Ifa*

Act One
Scene 1

WYNDEL BLACKMAN, a Black American aged early-thirties, and his mother MOMMA BLACKMAN have just arrived at the airport in an un-named W. African county. They and their luggage are in a booth where "he" is being questioned by a CUSTOM'S AGENT. There is a suitcase opened in front of the AGENT, and its contents spread in front of the AGENT. Other suitcases are also open, but their contents not spread. Included in those contents are three bags of gray/white powder, a book, and a framed photograph of a woman.

CUSTOM AGENT
So, you're travelling as a family, Mr. Blackman?

MOMMA
Correct. We sure is.

CUSTOMS AGENT
You, your mother, and your father: is that correct?

WYNDEL
I suppose you could say that.

MOMMA
Why you asking these questions? Don't you got nothin' better—

CUSTOMS AGENT
(*Interrupting*)
Well, I see your passport and your mother's but where is your father's?

WYNDEL
He doesn't need one.

MOMMA
No he don't!

CUSTOMS AGENT
Sir, everybody entering our country is required to present a passport unless they are a citizen in which case—

WYNDEL
(*Interrupting*)
He isn't a citizen although my mother might dispute that with me.

MOMMA
Boy, you know he comes from here. We done proved that with science. We tested your DNA to prove it.

CUSTOMS AGENT
He has to present proof of citizenship.

WYNDEL
Like I said, he isn't exactly a citizen and he don't have to have a passport.

CUSTOMS AGENT
Mr. Blackman, your father needs to be a citizen or he must have a passport.

MOMMA
Not if he be dead he don't.

WYNDEL
We brought him with us but he isn't here—not in the way you mean. He hasn't been here for a few months now. But we have brought him back, back to his homeland. Least that's what my mother says. She says,
(*Mimicking her voice*)
"This here's his home and we got ta bring him home."

CUSTOMS AGENT
I see. So he is with you in spirit, but not in person. That I suppose makes sense although it would have been easier if you....
(*Picks up one of the bags of gray/white powder from the suitcase*)
However, there is another problem. So, Mr. Blackman, do you think that you can bring drugs into our country and not get caught? Do you know the penalty for drug smuggling?

WYNDEL
(*Laughs*)
I told her it was stupid. "Momma," I said, "they aren't gonna let us bring those ashes into no country and scatter them." Course, did she listen? No, sir. She never does. Just "We gotta take your Daddy

home." Home, Jesus, the man grew up in Mississippi and moved to Cincinnati when he was grown. Never been out of the U.S. of A. except once and that was by accident. He and his buddy, Uncle George, were driving George's car to San Diego. Got lost in El Paso. They went across the border by accident. He told me that story when I was a teen. Says,

(*Imitating his father's voice*)

"Two Black men trying to get back into Texas. Took most of a day 'cause we had to be carryin' drugs. Wyndel, if there's one thing you need to know, boy, it's two Black men doin' anything the cops gonna stop ya and look for them drugs."

Sir, those aren't drugs. They are my father's ashes. That's what I was talking about. We're taking them to scatter where his great-great-grandfather come from. The slavers took him and dragged him off when he was just a teenager. That was almost two hundred years ago. I don't know where he was buried. Don't know where his great-grandfather was buried neither. His grandfather? Well, he's in Mississippi, right in the cemetery next to the Black Baptist Church. My Granny and Uncle Luke, they're in the same place, right next to. But, Momma, she says, "No, sir,—

MOMMA

(*Interrupting*)

My Matthew's goin' home, home where he belong. Do you know his people was royalty, kings and queens, over here? That's what his daddy tell him and what his daddy's daddy told him before. They was royalty!

CUSTOMS AGENT
(*Waving one of the plastic bags in the air*)
So, you say this powder is not drugs?

WYNDEL
Hell no! If you don't believe me, try a snort.
(*Laughs and reaches for the bag, which the CUSTOMS AGENT pulls away*)
Just smell it. I bet you can still smell his feet. That man sure did have halitosis of the toes. My girlfriend, Margarita, she always laughed about it. She said, "His feet could *foomigate* the house." Maybe she was right. We never did have roaches or anything. Of course, that might have been more to do with Momma. Now, this woman can clean. "God don't like no dirt," is what she says. She always has been one to speak for the Almighty.

MOMMA
You hush up, Wyndel Blackman, Don't you go disrespectin' the lord.

CUSTOMS AGENT
(*Opens bag, takes bit of ash on finger, examines it, maybe tastes it*)
If these are not drugs, why did you bring them here?

WYNDEL
Like I told you, Momma say we got to bring him home. Home to Africa. Got to bring them ashes here and spread them out where he should have been born. She did a whole lot of studying on it. Had some company studying his DNA. Even got the Mormons helping; although I doubt it was something they wanted to do. Figured out which ship that first great, greatarrived in Baltimore and then how he

was shipped to New Orleans. Once that woman decides something needs doing, there's no way she's going to stop till it's done

MOMMA
You could do the same—

CUSTOMS AGENT
(*Interrupting*)
(*Taking another bag and then another from the suitcase opened in front of him*)
This is your entire father?

WYNDEL
That's what Mr. Hemphil—he did the cremating—said. Course he put Daddy in a nice urn, but Momma said there weren't no sense in carryin' that on the plane. "Them folks in Africa don't need no funeral urns," she said.
    Me. I said, "They don't need no ashes neither." But she doesn't care about that or anything else I say. I tell her it's gonna cost us a lot of money and how I'd rather go to Hawaii, but she just says we got to take him home.So here we are. Yep, them bags are my father atleast all that's left of him.

MOMMA
All 'cept his soul. That's in a better place.

CUSTOMS AGENT
But, as I understand you, this is not his home.

WYNDEL

I know that and you know that, but Momma, she doesn't know it. She says there are three kinds of home. There's the home of the feet, the home of the head, and the home of the heart. The feet home, well, that's your roots. Like for me, my roots are in Cincinnati. That's where I grew up. I know that city like my hand. Feels good walking down the street because I belong there. The head, that's where it makes sense. Like when Daddy left Mississippi and moved to Ohio. He didn't want to work on a farm, share-cropping for a life. He wanted something better for himself and his children. His best friend went to San Diego, but Daddy he went to Cincinnati. Got himself a job and a wife. That was good enough for him. I reckon it's good enough for most men. But then there's the heart. A man's heart got yearnings. Someplace he just wants to be even though it don't make a lick of sense. Maybe he's never been there but that don't stop him for wanting. Like me. I think I'd like Hawaii. I think I'd like all that water and those beaches. Maybe I'd just lie on a beach and wait for the tide to drift me off to someplace else where I haven't never been and ain't never gonna come back from. Momma says Daddy was the same, always dreaming of someplace he just wanted to be. According to her he was dreaming of here, of Africa. She says this is the home of his heart. That's why we have to bring him home; got to bring him back to his home where he'd never been.

CUSTOMS AGENT
I know of no restrictions on bringing these ashes into our country, but I am not sure how the people in your ancestors' village will feel about spreading them. You know, they do not have to take him in. They do not have to welcome you and your

mother. A man may call one country or another home, but will he be welcome? That we cannot know.

FADE TO BLACK

Act One
Scene 2

WYNDEL's hotel room. It is at best a two-star hotel. He has taken a shower and is sitting on the bed in pants, but either no shirt or sleeveless undershirt. He is typing on his laptop. There may be a fan, but certainly no air conditioning. The suitcase from Scene 1 sits to one side. The photograph is on the small table next to the bed. Next to it his cell-phone and a book about computers or finance.
There's a knock on the door.

WYNDEL
(*Loudly*)
Leave me alone.

Lock turns and MOMMA enters

MOMMA
You feelin' better?

WYNDEL
I told you I want some time to—

MOMMA
(*Interrupting*)
Sleep is what you said. Rest up. Seems to me you've been on your computer. What were you doing? Emailing that floozy?

WYNDEL

Margarita's not a floozy and, no, I wasn't emailing her. Well, I did, but mostly I'm just thinking.

MOMMA
About what?

WYNDEL
About that customs guy…about this place… about everything. I mean would you believe they thought those ashes were drugs? I didn't expect that, not being a Black man here. I figured if I were White maybe they'd be questioning me, making sure they really were ashes. But, hell, I'm African American.

I was hoping… Hell, Momma, I was hoping I'd feel at home, like I belonged. You know, all my life I've been like guilty of being black, of walking while black, of playing basketball while being black, of driving while being black. Hell, even dating a Latina while being black. I couldn't get away from it, like it covered me.
(*He rubs his arm*)

Hell, it does cover me. … I figured here I'd fit in. Here I wouldn't feel.
(*Pause*)

Then I'd feel guilty about feeling guilty. Damn, it's the same here. Only difference isn't that I'm too dark. It's more like I'm too light. Then I feel like they're different, like I'm the one who's—I don't know—the one who looks right. It's like I spent my whole life trying to say color doesn't matter, and now I figure it does and it doesn't and I don't—

MOMMA

14

(*Interrupting*)
You is who you is. Same as everybody. You just need to find your roots. When we finish with your Daddy maybe you'll have figured it out. Maybe you'll find yourself here.

WYNDEL
Maybe I will and maybe I'll just be as confused as... Oh, shit, what's the use?

MOMMA
You told me you were going to rest up. Did you take a nap?

WYNDEL
I tried to.But this room, this bed! Anyway, I took a shower and—

MOMMA
(*Interrupting*)
If you'd agreed to share—

WYNDEL
(*Interrupting*)
You knew that wasn't ever happening. No way; no how. I'm too big to share a room with my mother.

MOMMA
Then don't go complaining about the accommodations.

WYNDEL

Accommodations. I don't see no accommodations around here. Have you tried your bed? Feels like somebody stuck rocks in there. Not hard. Just bumps. Damn, I could hardly—

MOMMA
Are you going to complain or you going to cope?

WYNDEL
(*Laughs*)
How many times have you asked me that? I've done enough coping for ten people. You know I have. How do you think I got that education you and Daddy were always going on at. College and a job, a real job, not just some nigger job but something a White man might do. A real job with papers and numbers not just using my back. Wasn't that coping? Don't go trying a guilt trip on me. I just got to look at my skin and feel enough guilt for just being alive.
(*He again rubs his arm*)

MOMMA
What you complaining about. Your Daddy and me, we worked damned hard so's you could get somewhere not just be another dumb nigger.

WYNDEL
I know it. I know you did, and it paid off. I workin' in an office sound like a White man, just like a White man. Wasn't that the plan?

And the people I work for? That's what they want. I'm the house nigger. "See how forward we are? How progressive. We got a real, life Black man working here." Truth is, if I start jiving and hooding it,

16

they'd get rid of me fast as that door can open. Affirmative action's fine if the Black man has a degree in literature and can quote himself some fancy French poetry. I'm not a Black man to them; I'm an Oreo. Just acting the way they want.

MOMMA
And, you think it's ok you playacting? Hiding who you are behind them fancy words? You think that's what we wanted?

WYNDEL
Who isn't acting? Who isn't passing one way or another. I never heard my Daddy speak out. He'd say all he wanted in our house or in the barbershop, but did he ever tell a White man what was what? No, sir, he didn't. He just played it cool, said yes, sir, and no, sir, and never argued. Then he'd go down to Sam's and he'd sit in one of them chairs while Sam cut his hair and he'd talk to them other Niggers and they'd jive and talk and holy shit the shit they'd tell each other like it was true. Of course, you never heard none of that. I don't think you would have liked Daddy when he was at Sam's. But down there, Daddy would run his mouth and pass different. It's all an act. His, mine, yours, too, if you want to be honest.

MOMMA
And, you think the people here care? You think they know you doing an act or not? They don't care about acts. They don't care—

WYNDEL
(Interrupting)

17

Yeah, your act, too. Even coming here. You think I don't know all of this is part act, too? You think I don't know what you want? I ain't that dumb, Momma. When I was little, well, I didn't always catch on; but that was years back. Now, I read you. I read you like that book over there.

(*He gestures to the book on his table.*)

MOMMA
You brought that here? Why? That's—

WYNDEL
(*Interrupting*)
It's just a book. What—

MOMMA
(*Interrupting. While speaking she moves to the bedside table*)
Not the book. Who gives a damn about a book? This!
(*She holds up the photograph and then throws it onto the bed*)

WYNDEL
Why not? I love her. She loves me. When we get done with this act of yours, she and I are getting married. Day after we get back, it's down to the court house and we get hitched. You can come or not. You can be happy or not. We're still... See, that's what I mean by you playing your part. Momma, didn't you know I'd figure it out. Bringing Daddy's ashes back to Africa. Back home. This isn't his home.
(*He puts the photo back in place*)

You want me to find my roots. That's what you want. Hell, you think I don't know? You know the funny thing. Maybe we can trace something of Daddy back to here, but you act like there's no white blood in him, me, or you. Of course, there is. You saw the DNA report. You're the one who spent the money on it, not me. You read it, too. You know. Seventy-five percent African. You think the other twenty-five just jumped into my genes by themselves? You think there hasn't been a White woman or maybe a White man along the way?

MOMMA
Slaves didn't get a choice. That doesn't mean they cheated.

WYNDEL
Cheated?! On what? Their race? Themselves? Of course, nobody cheated.
(*He picks up the photo again and shows some affection towards it*)
    Besides, aren't you asking me to cheat? Aren't you hoping I'll fall in love with some…with what? Some Nubian princess or something? You think I'm going to walk into a village in the middle of nowhere and find my soul mate? Are you nuts?

MOMMA
Not your soul mate; not even a woman. I want you to look in the mirror, the real mirror, the one that shows who you are.

WYNDEL
And who the hell is that?

19

MOMMA
A proud man. Proud of his heritage. Proud of his skin. Proud of his education and his abilities. Somebody who doesn't fake his words and doesn't sell his heart for a pink skin.

WYNDEL
Is that what you think I'm doing, selling out? I love her. Margarita's a good woman.

BLACK OUT

ACT One
Scene 3

AKIN's room somewhere in the heart of the city. The room is shabby, clearly its occupant is poor. The major furniture in the room is the bed at the left side of the room. There is a small reading table to the right with some books on it. AKIN runs around from one spot to the other stuffing a sack-like-bag with any available food in the room.

There is a sound at the door. As the door opens SEGUN enters. He is carrying a heavy sack. SEGUN speaks with a heavy Yoruba accent.

SEGUN
Waka fast fast make we go. They are waiting.

AKIN
But father, must I go?

SEGUN,
You must go oh! See? You must go Kogi because na you know Kogi. You go University for Kogi. You must help your father go Kogi.

AKIN
Father, I have things to do. Going to Kogi will hinder—

SEGUN
(Interrupting)
What are you want to do? Anything you are do now will not help.

21

AKIN

Why father? Why will it not help?

SEGUN

Because I am give the car to you.

AKIN

What do you want me to do with the car?

SEGUN

Drive it. Drive like me.Carry passengers, and make for money. See? Every somebody needs money to be happy. See? The car gives you money. See? Then you find wife and have children.

AKIN

I've already told you again and again, Father. I want to start a troupe, I studied Theatre Arts not taxi driving; I am an artist.

SEGUN

You want troop, you go to jungle find baboon. You want money, you find way to make it. All the time you are talk of artist, artist. What are you gain by it? Artist make nice dance and song. Artist maybe paint picture. Not make money. Not feed children.

AKIN

I'm a performer. That's who I am. Why did you pay my fees through school? You did that so that my life can be better. I need to do

22

something to help you. To improve the economy of the family. As an actor I will earn money, enough money to take of all our bills.

SEGUN
Akin my boy, I am send you to school to help me, good, very very good. You see? You are help me by go to Kogi. The man, American is get plenty money, is carry many many bags. Is a big man with one Momma who is get plenty money too. We take them go Kogi, we get plenty money Akin, that is how to help the family. When we go Kogi you learn how to become driver. See?

AKIN
Fine, I'll go to Kogi with you but, father, I will never become a driver. I have my own dreams. I am going to Kogi only to please you. Going with you this one time.

SEGUN
If you are not be a driver who are you want to be?

AKIN
I told you, I'm an artist, a theatre artist. Someday, I want to have my own dance troupe. That is what an artist does.

SEGUN
Fine, fine, you dance. Bring customer to taxi. Like man with monkey that dance to bring coin. Come and carry bag make we go. You are not grow up to know life finish yet.

AKIN

(Exiting the room and shouting his lines to SEGUN)
Father, you take the bag. I have to tell friends that I am travelling to Kogi. I will meet you at the park.

SEGUN
Your friends is advice you bad bad. They is advice you to dance because you school university. Who dance help for Africa? Go fast fast and come to meet me there oh!
(Carries the bag and exits behind AKIN)

Light Out

ACT One

Scene 4

Light reveals the rear of a taxi. WYNDEL and MOMMA pace behind the automobile. Their suitcases are piled nearby. Neither SEGUN or AKIN are present. SEGUN enters bearing two sacks and drops them in front of MOMMA who jerks away from the bags towards WYNDEL. SEGUN does an elaborate greeting movement, which his son will imitate later in the scene.

MOMMA

Now, what might all that be?

SEGUN

Bags... Ghana-Must-Go

WYNDEL

What the hell is it for?

SEGUN

T'ings for me and me son, Akin. The journey is long, very long trip. Such trip requires preparation. The snail carries its house anywhere it travels. Do you know reason? It cannot—

MOMMA

(*Interrupting*)

I hope we aren't going to wait for your son all day. We haven't got that time.

SEGUN

Man from hotel say your name Blackman. Good name… very good name. Anything not black, bad. Black is beautiful, see? Black is good. See? Don't disagree. So, Mrs. Blackman, talk about have time or have no time, be patient. Calm your head down. Patient people gain long life…plenty long life and plenty everything. See? It is little by small, small that bird builds its nest. See? We shall get there but be patient. Have time. See? We go like snail, slow, slow.

WYNDEL
(*Moves over to MOMMA*)
What is this man saying? Snails and birds and all… Oh my God… What have we—

MOMMA
(*Interrupting*)
Wyndel, you just calm down. Just breathe easy and take a breath. Let me take care of it. Remember, Baby, you're doing this for your daddy.

WYNDEL
No, Momma, I'm not doing this for my Daddy. He's dead and he doesn't care, least not any more. I doubt he'd care even if he wasn't dead. I'm doing it for you. To please you so you can get it, get that I love Margarita; that I'm going to be hers, just like you were with Daddy and just like he was with you. I have told you and told you that I'm not a kid anymore. Your hope that I 'm going to fall in love with some Black girl, that I'm going to find my true love here in Africa, that my feelings for Margarita will be as scattered as his ashes. Coming to Africa isn't about Daddy's ashes and it isn't about finding

26

no roots. It's about getting you to back off. Maybe not a lot, but some, please, just a little.

MOMMA

You're too young to know what love is. More important, how you gonna love somebody before you love yourself and your own roots.

WYNDEL

If a Black man needs to love his roots before he can love himself no wonder we're killing ourselves so fast in America. But, not everybody is, Momma. Do you know why? Because roots aren't real. We aren't plants. We aren't trees. We move around, Momma. We move and move. Maybe some folks were forced to move, maybe they were moved in chains, but they still moved and they don't have what you're calling roots nor memories. Want to talk about my roots? They're in Cincinnati, Ohio, U.S. of A. My roots? The Reds, maybe the Bengals. My best memory, sitting in right field with Daddy and catching that baseball. A homerun ball and I caught it. Now that's a memory. It may not be the best place in the world, especially if you're skin ain't the right color, but it's where—

MOMMA
(*Interrupting*)
There's always a root, a root for all us Blacks in America... we may all think ourselves Americans but we're not. We're from here. This is our place. It is in our bones, in our genes. We are one with this, with Africa... this is—

SEGUN

(*Interrupting*)
Ehm, don't worry, Akin come here now...very soon. Then we go to Idah.

WYNDEL
What's so special about your son coming with you... I mean with us? What's so special about it?

SEGUN
Ah Mr. Blackman, this Africa O! Yes, this Africa. We not take things for granted here. To farm with old worn-out hoe is to go without new one. The wolf of your country no go break your bone. My son graduate University near Idah... Anyigba, yes the place is Anyigba. Akin know Idah. Akin guide us to Idah. Son know what father not.

WYNDEL
(*Directed to MOMMA but said as if to SEGUN*)
Glad you recognize what your son knows. Some parents...
(*Looking at his watch and then continuing directly to SEGUN*)
    Well then, he should be here. I want to get this ashes thing done and head back home from this hell. And, yes, Momma, I want to get back to Margarita. I miss her and I miss the fucking.

MOMMA
Wyndel Blackman, you mind your language!

WYNDEL
(*Mopping his brow*)
Momma, I have to get out of here. The heat is unbearable...

MOMMA
You know it ain't about no heat... it's about you being in heat for that girl. Can't you take her out of your head just once? For your Daddy?

WYNDEL
There you go again Momma—

SEGUN
(*Interrupting*)
Here Akin come. Look, Akin fine man. My son, handsome man. Is Akin not handsome man?

AKIN
(*Yoruba style of greeting and speaking in the same accent but better grammar than SEGUN*)
Welcome to Africa.

MOMMA
Thanks a load, but we don't need formalities. We need to get moving. Your father says we have a long way to travel.

SEGUN
Akin, is graduate. Studied Theatre Arts from University.
(*To AKIN*)
    Tell Mr. Blackman about studies. Tell him about the Igala nation.

WYNDEL

I'm not really interested. Let's get going. Get into that cab and let's roll. This heat is killing me.

MOMMA
Don't be rude, Wyndel. I'm sure we can learn a great deal from Akin. Isn't that right, Mr. Segun?

SEGUN
No, Mr. Blackman, one must look for something where they are found. I be old man. My son, Akin, is the eyes of me. We go to Idah, home of Igala people. Me, I no know Idah; but Akin, Idah is like palm of hand. He must tell before we go.

WYNDEL
Momma, can't we just get another taxi?

MOMMA
Don't be so impatient. We should listen to him. I'm sure Mr. Segun knows what he doing.

SEGUN
Thank you, Madam Blackman. It is good to be patient. The person that get patience get all t'ings. Patience is juice of life, father of all virtues. Akin, tell them.

AKIN
We are going to Kogi State. We are going to the kingdom of Igala people. You must have heard of Princess Inikpi who chose to die to save the Igala from war. We are going to her land.

WYNDEL
Are you done talking, Brother?

AKIN
Brace up, sir. We are taking a long trip. It is like going to the end of the world from this very spot. It is going to be a very long journey, sir.

SEGUN
How long journey, my son?

AKIN
Very far, father…it is like the distance from here to Ibadan in ten places. A very long journey my father.

WYNDEL
Momma, if it's do damn far, why don't we just fly?

AKIN
There is no airport there.

MOMMA
From the sky we will see nothing. From the clouds we will learn nothing of our roots.

WYNDEL
I could see those clouds. Nothing wrong with that. We saw them plenty on the way here.

(Yelling at suitcase)

Hear that, Daddy, no airport so we're forced to travel by land. Wouldn't you prefer being back in Cincinnati?

AKIN
There is no two ways about it.

WYNDEL
Then let's get going. If it's so far, shouldn't we be on our way?

SEGUN
Wait yet. There are things we are not talk yet. We must agree on somet'ing before we go. My son, Akin, talk say we are going end of the world. We must take care of car on way. You see, this is old car. It was given to me by father. I have to take care of car, give car to Akin.

AKIN
(Muttering to himself)
And, give it to me he will, no matter what I want.

WYNDEL
What does he need it for with that fancy education of his?

AKIN
(Again to himself)
At least this American gets it.

SEGUN

In Africa, education good for head and good for heart, not help take care of stomach. Africa not Cincinnati; Cincinnati different, Africa different. See?

MOMMA
Mr. Segun, what's your point. Take care of this. Take care of that. Get to your point. Your son has said it is going to be a long journey. We don't have all day.

WYNDEL
Momma, if you don't understand the man, let him go. We don't need to use his damn cab. After all it isn't the only one around.

SEGUN
Akin, can you hear? Mr. Blackman is not thinking like Black man. See? To be called a monkey, first monkey must learn to climb tree. This Africa... Yes, Mr. Blackman. Yes, Momma Blackman. In Africa we behave African. See? If you want go Idah by another motor, the road is there. Go! Go your way. Find your route to Idah. See? Akin my son, let us go.

MOMMA
Hold on, Mr. Segun. It hasn't come to that. Least, not yet. I haven't understood you. I want to; I want to understand you.

WYNDEL
No, Momma, let him go. America's a free country; in Cincinnati no one has to talk the cab driver into giving him a ride. A wave of the hand and the guy stops. You get in and off you go.

SEGUN

Mr. Blackman, this Africa not America, not your Cincinnati or Cincinnation or Cincin anything. You see? This Africa, In Africa we bargain; we talk price before we go Idah. You see? The way that is marked for good performance outside must first show its skills at home. Mr. Blackman, if you not going to Igala kingdom with me and Akin, go your way.

MOMMA

Just what are we negotiating?

SEGUN

The pay... the money you pay me...and my son. See?

MOMMA

Mr. Segun, we talked before. We agreed... Aren't we done negotiating the price?

SEGUN

No, Woman, we never do yet. You see, for the hunter's dog to hunt well well for hunting time the hunter must give him food well well for eating time. See? We go on long journey, long journey to end of world, so we must talk price again. The car does not walk on empty stomach like warrior...soldier. See? It drinks fuel. I no get fueling station. I be poor man. I must buy petrol. I must feed car. See?

WYNDEL

So, what's the con? How much are we talking about? How much do you expect us to pay?

SEGUN
Double of what we agreed. Yes, double because we now go to end of world. See?

WYNDEL
We're not paying! ... That's outrageous!

MOMMA
Hush, Baby. You leave this to me. Of course, we is payin'. We is payin' the man and then we is going.

WYNDEL
Momma, are you nuts? Is that what you call bargaining, just giving in that way?

MOMMA
Wyndel, in Rome you behave like you is a Roman. This here is Africa not America. This ain't Cincinnati.

WYNDEL
It sure isn't Cincinnati.
(To himself)
    And it sure as hell isn't bargaining.

AKIN

We are already running out of time. We must be on the way now. We are stopping over at Akure.

WYNDEL
Stopping? Why? What the hell for?

AKIN
(*Picks the bags and moving towards the car*)
For a rest... and food. Maybe something good happen there.

LIGHTS FADE

ACT one
Scene 5
Akure. Sun is setting. The car comes to a stop at a roadside park.
Traders display wares at random while others hawk about. Distant
calls to prayers blast over a loud speakers. WYNDEL, SEGUN,
MOMMA, and AKIN are in the vehicle. Other vehicles are also
parked with drivers and loaders calling for customers.

AKIN opens the door and jumps out of the vehicle, a half-
consumed bottle of water in hand and gulps. The others, more
sluggishly, open their respective doors and move towards centre
stage. SEGUN takes the centre stage. WYNDEL and MOMMA
stand close to each other. They are exhausted.

WYNDEL
(*Shouting towards AKIN who is still drinking his bottle of water*)
How long the hell do we have to bake in this shit-hole taxi?

AKIN
(*Throws the bottle away*)
In some more hours we shall be approaching Kogi. We are almost
there.

WYNDEL
(*Stands up and moves towards AKIN quizzically*)
Some more hours. Some more hours. What does that mean? How
long is some?
(*Turning towards MOMMA*)
    Momma I ain't going any *further* than here.
(*Shouting towards the direction of the car*)

37

Daddy, can you hear that? I ain't going any *further!* I don't want to die in some hell-hot-baked shitty taxi. America's a good place to die. Daddy, I ain't dying in some African hell for the sake of returning your ashes to their roots. Roots? What were you, some kind of tree? Hell, your roots were in Mississippi. You want me to take you back there? That'll do me just fine. You want to go back to Nogales? I'll take you back across the border to Mexico. Sure, I'll let the border patrol check me for damn drugs. I may be Black, but I'm a dumb nigger and I'm going to die for your ashes.

MOMMA
(*Goes to WYNDEL and tries to drag him upstage center*)
Baby, you are losin' it. You're plumb out of control. What'll these men think of you. Get yourself a grip and a bottle of that water. The man says we's almost there and so we's almost there. Now you get a grip, young man. You hearin' me?

WYNDEL
Momma, I think you've brought me here to suffer and die. You'd rather I'd be dead than with the woman I love. Well, if you get your wish, take my ashes back to my roots, to America...to Cincinnati. Take them back to Margarita. But Momma, I am not just laying down and dying, not without putting up a fight. I'mnot going anywhere *further.* Not in this vehicle that stinks like hell and is trying to bake us to death.

MOMMA
Pshaw. You get a grip, Wyndel Blackman. You just get yourself a grip.

SEGUN
(*Angrily*)
Car don't stink hell! Blackman, car no get problem! It is road…bad road! The road is no good. The road kill car. The government is no do good road. The car is suffer for bad road.

WYNDEL
(*Charging in anger towards SEGUN but MOMMA tries to hold him back. SEGUN also charges towards WYNDEL. AKIN and MOMMA stand between SEGUN and WYNDEL*)
How the heck is that my business? Your bad government and your bad roads aren't my business. We're paying for a safe trip. You're getting paid well for it. We aren't paying with some death wish in mind.

MOMMA
Baby, let the poor man be. The problem ain't his. He's doin' best he can like everybody. You got your mind set against Africa. You can't be seeing nothin' good here. Can't see the good in people like Segun. Do you realize—

WYNDEL
(*Interrupting*)
Damn it, Momma! There ain't nothing good here. I miss home. I miss my woman. I—

AKIN
(*Interrupting*)

39

Mr. Blackman, is it the distance or the bad road? What is wrong?

WYNDEL
Everything! The distance, bad road, the heat…

MOMMA
Yes, it's the heat, your heat for Margarita, but, Boy, you bury that heat for the sake of this journey.

AKIN
We all need to calm down and be prospective about the journey ahead. We are almost there. Igala Kingdom is not too far from here.

MOMMA
Wyndel, why don't you walk around a bit. Maybe you'll find a souvenir, something to take home to Margarita. Seems to me you need a bit of air 'fore we get back in Mr. Segun's taxi.

AKIN
I will go with you to help barter if you wish.

WYNDEL
Okay, I'll look around. Like there's going to be something I want to bring back to my girl besides me. Then we go, right? Let's get the hell out of here.

SEGUN

Mr. Blackman, why do you like hell too much? You talk hell, talk hell all the time. Are you citizen of hell? Hell is no good place. Fire everywhere inside hell burn people. Hell is no good place at all.

WYNDEL

If I didn't like hell, I sure wouldn't be here.
(*to Akin*)
 Come on, Brother, show me where I can buy a love potion.

(*WYNDEL and AKIN move away*)

MOMMA

Segun, why have we stopped here? What are we doing here?

SEGUN

Good ma'am, we are stop to eat food…we are stop to rest too. After rest we go to Igala Kingdom.

MOMMA

But, Mr. Segun, you have food in your bag. We don't have to stop for food.

SEGUN

Food in bag is not as good as we buy here. Don't you want something that taste good? Don't you want cool drinks?

MOMMA

What I want is for my son to find what he needs here.

SEGUN
Your son needs love potion?

MOMMA
(*Laughs bitterly*)
No. That's the one thing Wyndel don't need. He's always been good
with the ladies. It's with himself he's got trouble. He needs to figure
out who he is, where he's going in his life. I'm his mother and I see
how he ain't got no sense of himself and it grieves me, Mr. Segun. It
surely does. A parent can see the road ahead because she's already
done travelled the one behind. I didn't really come here to spread
Matthew's ashes. Oh, I figure he'd want that, too. But, mostly I want
our boy to figure out what life's about. It ain't just chasing this gal
and that.

SEGUN
Every parent worry about his children. I worry about Akin. He wants
to be an actor, a dancer. How make family that way? I want him take
my taxi. My father gave it to me. It is what I have to pass on. It is
what I have so he is my son.

MOMMA
Matthew worried that way about Wyndel. Said a son should be the
continuation of the father. I don't know what that means about us
mothers, but I do know that young men need to figure out who they
is and who they is trying to be.

SEGUN

They talk big talk and dream big dream but t'ing is they can only do what can be done.

MOMMA
That sure is the truth. But can they accept it?

(*MOMMA and SEGUN are both shaking their heads as AKIN and WYNDEL come back up to them.*)

WYNDEL
OK, I looked around. Nothing worth buying here.
(*He pokes AKIN*)
     Not a good love potion in the place.

AKIN
That is so. But there is good fruit and bread.

WYNDEL
Hey, man, we can eat what your Daddy got in his bag. Let's get this over with.

SEGUN
(*To AKIN*)
We do as Mr. Blackman talk. Let us go Igala Kingdom. We eat food inside car. We drink bottle of water inside car.

All characters are about to go into the car but a young lady (UFEDO) runs to meet them. She is a beautiful young woman.

43

UFEDO
Good afternoon.

WYNDEL
(*Suddenly aware of her he takes a second look and then a third before responding*)
Yes, yes. Good afternoon.

SEGUN
Good afternoon, young lady.

UFEDO
(*Speaks to WYNDEL and smiles broadly at him; WYNDEL smiles in response*)
Please, are you going to Kogi?

AKIN
(*His immediate attraction to UFEDO should be obvious*)
Yes, we are. That is our destination.

UFEDO
I am Ufedo. I am going to Kogi, too. Do you mind lifting me?

SEGUN
(*To MOMMA*)
Ma'am, this girl going to Kogi. Can we going together?

MOMMA
Why are you asking me? Ain't we uncomfortable enough?

SEGUN

To help... Is good to help. The right hand clean the left hand, the left hand clean the right hand. See? Two hands clean. See? Help good well well.

MOMMA

That's all well and good if there's enough water for washing. But I don't know about there being enough of anything here.

WYNDEL

(*Looking UFEDO over carefully and with some measure of desire*)
Momma, that ain't like you. It ain't Christian at all. What would Daddy think if we turned this nice lady down? Why his ashes will never forgive us. They'll be blowing around in the wind and stirring the dust with indignation if we don't help her. Ain't that right, Mr. Segun? Ain't that right, my brother Akin.

SEGUN

Yes, Mr. Blackman, I the sure the spirit of your father go—

MOMMA

(*Interrupting*)
But, Wyndel, the smell...the heat...the car is already overloaded and the roads are bad.

AKIN

I'm sure we can—

WYNDEL
(*Interrupting*)
Of course, we can. It's only some more hour. Ain't that what you said?

(*To UFEDO*)
Ufedo. Is that your name.

(*UFEDO nods*)
Sure is pretty. Why don't you get into this here car and let's get going?
(*He holds one of the back doors of the taxi open and UFEDO moves next to him*)

SEGUN
Thank you, sir. See? Help good well well.

UFEDO
(*Turning and bending as she greets*)
Thank you so much ma'am, sir…

WYNDEL
Get on in. Like the man said, "We got some hours to go."

MOMMA
Baby!

WYNDEL
Momma, you get on in, too. We ain't got no time to waste.

SEGUN
Oya! Every somebody, inside the car. We go Kogi now.

WYNDEL
(*He is the last to enter the back seat of the cab. It ends up with UFEDO in middle between him and MOMMA. His line is delivered without conviction and he looks at UFEDO while he delivers it.*)
The faster we get to Kogi, the faster I get back to Cincinnati and to Margarita. I sure am ready…

SIGUN
Man often hurry place he not want be go too slow to place is good. Some hour more, we see. Well, well.

SEGUN is the last to get into the cab. He closes the door.
The engine starts and

LIGHTS FADE

47

ACT One
Scene 6
Inside taxi. Night. SEGUN is driving but is nodding off at the wheel. AKIN sits next to him occasionally reaching over to touch his father or otherwise make sure he is awake. WYNDEL sits behind SEGUN. He is looking out the window, but taking occasional side-glances at UFEDO who sits between him and MOMMA, who is watching out the window. Since this is a British car, the driver should be on the right and the presentation of the stage should be such that SEGUN and WYNDEL are more downstage.

On a screen to the passenger side of the car, a small heard of antelope are seen bounding past.

MOMA
Did you see that? What are them things running out there?

SEGUN
Not to be frightened, Madam Momma. Antelope not dangerous. Good to eat. See? If we carry gun, I shoot and take meat to offer to god in Igala Kingdom. Sacrifice go make Daddy's soul go easy easy. Make chief happy well well to say 'Daddy's soul welcome to Kogi'.

WYNDEL
Isn't there some rule or something about hunting and rifles? You can't just go around shooting something whenever you please.

AKIN

Why not? This is Africa not your America. We hunt here. Lion hunt. Man hunt. Antelope die. What is left hyena eat. Buzzard eat. Life goes on. That is nature of t'ings. God writes the play and we all have a part. We are all actors in the theatre of life. Antelope maybe not like part where we shoot, but maybe like better than lion eat.

WYNDEL

Are you serious, man? You got lions here?! Serious lions? The king of the jungle and all that shit?

AKIN

Yes. We have lions. They—

UFEDO

(*Interrupting*)

What is men so about lion. Lion is a lazy animal. It let women do the work. They hunt while he watches. Only thing he does is to roar. Make big roar and that scare. But women do work.

MOMMA

(*Chuckles*)

Like men. Lots of roaring but not much action.

WYNDEL

Hey, I get lots of action. You ask Margarita if I don't.

MOMMA

(*Laughs loudly*)

UFEDO
(*As she speaks, WYNDEL is watching her*)
The leopard is better than lion. She is the Queen of jungle. Hunts all
by herself. It is hard to be seen. One has to look careful to see
leopard, but she is a great hunter. Whenever you see the leopard you
will love her. It is not like the lion making noise. Man, like gorilla beat
its chest and draws attention to himself. That why lion roar. The
Leopard needs no attention. She is the queen of the jungle. The zebra
know from who to run. The antelope know who they fear. Even the
gazelle who can run most fast is afraid when leopard come.

SEGUN
That is true. When leopard hunt, jungle is quiet. All animal stop
move. See? When lion hunt, jungle is noisy. All animal run to hide.
Same with every somebody. See? Man that talk well well make big
sound. Women hide. Man that no talk well well go talk, the women
watch and hear. That secret, Akin. That how you find good wife.

WYNDEL
Have you got a good wife, Segun?

SEGUN
Best wife. She have good look. She cook sweet. She give me pickin's.
She give to me Akin. He go school and make proud. Well well. What
more can man ask?

MOMMA
(*Turning to UFEDO*)

Well, I ain't one for that barefoot, pregnant and in the kitchen story. I figure a woman has a life, too. What do you think?

UFEDO
Woman has brain. Men think with desire. Woman guide the man…teaches him how to live. First, trap then teach. The man thinks he is the lion, thumps his chest like gorilla. The woman teaches him how to be dog.

MOMMA
Amen! I like your spirit, Girl.

WYNDEL
Momma, you never had Daddy on no leash.

MOMMA
And how would you know?

WYNDEL
(*Flustered*)
He told me. He'd talk. Down at Sam's Barber Shop. He'd sit there with a hot towel on his face and he'd tell stories 'bout being a lover and how you thought you were calling the shots but…

SEGUN
When man talk to other men he talk big. He not always tell true. Am I not talk true, Momma Blackman?

UFEDO

When woman marry, she must respect the husband. He must respect her, too. Man and woman must learn to respect one another. Not respect between husband and wife then marry not real. Yes, must have respect.

(*She laughs*)

But first she must train him. He must know where to sleep. If he goes out at night, it means he is not well trained. If he goes after other ladies then he is also not well trained.

AKIN

So, how would you train that man of yours?

UFEDO

(*Patting WYNDEL on his leg and smiling at him*)

First you get his attention. You make him like and desire you. Then you give him treat, treat enough he want to please you. Then he behave good, you give him more. If he behaves badly, you ignore him. Every man wants good treatment. Most of all, man not like if woman ignore.

MOMMA

Ain't that the truth, girl.

SEGUN

And, you are start put baiting trap for man?

UFEDO

Trap always have bait. Patient, patient until the right man comes. Time moves like this taxi. Very slow...

SEGUN
We're going. We not slow. We soon get to Kogi.

WYNDEL
When? I'm awful tired of sitting, My ass is—

SEGUN
Not worry. We only some hours to go. See? Akin, no be so?

BLACK

ACT ONE
Scene 7

MORNING, outside the palace of ATA IGALA (Igala King). The palace is simply but beautifully built. There is a throne where the ATA will sit. Behind the throne, the skin of a lion is hung while at the footstool, two carved elephants stand on each side of the throne. Seats are arranged in a semi-circle. MOMMA BLACKMAN, WYNDEL, SEGUN, AKIN and UFEDO are on the chairs close to the throne. They and anyone else on stage sway to Igala music. WYNDEL has the bags of his father's ashes lying on the ground at his feet. WYNDEL pays less attention to the music and the elders than he does to UFEDO. When he catches her eye, he smiles and she smiles back. This continues until the ATA (KING) IGALA enters. A GUARD holds an umbrella over ATA's head. The king is tall and imposing. He carries a horsetail whisk. He makes his way to his throne, stopping to speak to people in the crowd, to greet small children, and in general to act like a royal and a politician. All activities stop and all stand to greet and remain thus until the ATA takes his seat. GUARD stands behind him. Just behind ATA enters his JESTER ACHIMI. ACHIMI mimics his master's actions. When the ATA is seated, the JESTER sits at his feet.

Once the JESTER sits, the priest OHIOGA enters from a different direction. He, too, makes a progress across the stage, solemnly making what the audience will imagine to be sacred gestures.

ALL except WYNDEL and MOMMA
(*WYNDEL, and MOMMA are still sitting. UFEDO urges them to stand.*)
Gaabaidu!

54

ATA

(*Sits comfortably before talking*)

Let the music continue. The ancestors are happy, why should we not be?

Music and other merriments resume. Lobs of kola nuts are passed round for everyone to pick. WYNDEL and MOMMA picks but do not do anything with them. After a while the king's jester, ACHIMI, steps forward to the centre of the semicircle, waves his hands and the merriment stops

ACHIMI

All greetings due to the king never elude the crown. Gaabaidu! ATA is the elephant, it trusts the size of its anus before it swallows the Odo fruit, seed and all. Gaabaidu! ATA is the solid rock that provides the needed ground for the elephant to stride upon. No matter how well an idol is made it must have something to stand upon. Gaabaidu! Your subjects greet you.

ATA

(*Waves his horse tail fly whisk around especially towards MOMMA and WYNDEL*)

I greet my subjects in the name of the ancestors. As they drove the usurpers from our land, let us celebrate their victory. Great are the people of Igala. Today is a day of joy, my people. It is not ordinary that we are here to welcome our people in this way. Yes, our people! A fowl does not forget where it lays its eggs. The *Ohioga* told me a long time ago after the consultation of *Ifa* that, a day like this would come. A farmer does not boast that he has had a good harvest until his stock of yams lasts till the following harvest. Before I proceed, I want us to know that we have our people with us. Let us formally meet them and know why they have come to see us. When they came to me yesterday and told me who they are and why they have come to our land. I told them to wait. It is good to share the joy together as a people. I have also invited the *Ohioga*, the priest of *Ifa*, to share in this good news. That is why we are here today.

UFEDO
(Turning and bending as she greets while she speaks, WYNDEL hangs on her every word)
Amideju! My fathers, ladies and gentlemen. I greet you in the name of the gods and our ancestors. When the ancestors want to use you, you become a tool in their hands. It is the fortunate person that the physician undertakes to help. You all know that I am your daughter, so, I am not strange to you. The plantain is much too common to be unknown to the farmer. These good people here with us,
(Pointing at them as she calls their names)
    Segun and his son, Akin, are not far from us. They are of the Yoruba origin. They have brought Wyndel Blackman and Momma Blackman from Lagos. They have come to country from America. These good people gave me lift from Akure to our land yesterday by the design of our ancestors. They have asked that I present them to you and to ask your permission to fulfill their mission. Amideju! While Akin and his father needs no introduction, let me allow Wyndel and Momma to introduce their selves and state their mission as well. I greet you once again, Amideju!

MOMMA
(*Stands and bows in greeting. While she speaks, WYNDEL looks away*)
Hello, your kingship. My son and I, we have brought my man, his
father, home to Africa. Home to his land and to his people who is
the same as your people. It was his wish to return to the land of his
ancestors, so my boy Wyndel and I done brought his ashes so they
could be home, so his heart could be home, so his soul could be at
rest.

ACHIMI
The she goat bleats while the Billy goat looks away.

AKIN
(*Pushing forward*)
Forgive her your highness; the ways of those from other lands are
not as ours. The mother speaks before her son. She does not know
that he who carries the spear has precedent over she who does not.
Momma Blackman speaks of her dead husband's wish. Would any
Igala not tell such a wish to his son?

MOMMA
(*Sputters*)
Are you saying I don't know what my husb—

SEGUN
(*Pushing forward and interrupting*)
Momma Blackman, my son, Akin, is talk that the ways of Cincinnati
not the ways Igala people. He is talk that before the ATA of the

57

Igala, the man talk first. The woman not talk until permission is given.

MOMMA
(*Pointing at UFEDO*)
So why did she get to talk? She ain't no warrior. Where her spear at?

ATA
(*Gestures to UFEDO to come to him.*
As ATA speaks, WYNDEL is at first startled and then angry.)
Ufedo is soon to be my third wife. She will be a queen among the Igala. She will bear the son I do not yet have and he will be ATA after me.

SEGUN
Gaabaidu! Great King of Igala kingdom, this woman she not know the Africa ways.

ACHIMI
Yet she comes here to ask something. It is a foolish antelope that comes to waterhole without first making sure the leopard is not waiting.
(*Turning to WYNDEL*)
   Speak, American. What do you wish from this great ATA?

WYNDEL
(*Comes forward with one of the bags of ashes in his hand.*
He is still upset about what UFEDO has said)

It ain't so much what I wish, King. It's what my Momma wants. She wants my father's ashes spread out here where his great-great-grandfather came from. She wants us to spread his ashes here so she can say we're African and not Black American. So we can say we ain't from slave folk but free.

(*He turns to UFEDO to say the next*)

Most of all, she wants me to say I'm an African so I won't marry Margarita. She's my girl back home in Cincinnati and Momma don't approve because she's a white gal.

(*Turning back to the ATA*)

So, King that's why we're here. Do you mind if we take these bags of his ashes and spread them around?

(*Once more turning to UFEDO*)

Once we've done that, we can get out of your hair, head back home to the states. No point in hanging around here is there.

OHIOGA

(*Stands with a start, walks about chanting some incantations. WYNDEL and MOMMA look at him quizzically. He faces ATA, bows in greetings before talking*)

Gaabaidu! The king of lions! The elephant that strides and wakes the sleeping forest. If I understand this young man very well, he has brought back the body of his late father who is of our origin. He has brought his father home for burial. That is good news. Yes, good news, because the ripe fruit will always drop under the mother-tree. But, what I do not understand is this talk of ashes. Your highness, is he saying that an abomination has been committed and our clan's man has been burnt to ashes? Such an act would be an affront to the gods.

MOMMA
What you talkin' about, fool. These are my husband's ashes. He was cremated right proper. Mr. Hemphil, he done said—

ACHIMI
Auntie, Auntie, why you speak to priest? You want curse on you? You want him curse so you not have baby.
(*He looks her over carefully*)
    Maybe better curse you have baby.
(*He laughs*)

WYNDEL
(*Throws the bag of ashes in his hand on the ground*)
This ain't no abomination! It's cremation. Momma had him cremated so we could bring him here, so we could spread his ashes where she thought he'd want them, here in Africa ... in Igala land. Since when is it wrong to honor your husband's wishes, to honor your father's wishes. He's here because...

OHIOGA
(*Laughs as he moves round WYNDEL in cycle. Suddenly stops and throws some cowries on the floor and look closely at the cowries for interpretations.*)
When the root of a tree begins to decay, it spreads death to the branches. Young man, we do not set a clan's man ablaze for whatever reason. Burn a clan's man to ashes? Our deeds carry consequences, consequences that are hardly confined to our lives. Your highness, the land has been polluted. The polluted land must be cleansed at once.

60

WYNDEL

(*Angrily moving towards MOMMA*)

Momma, what are these folks talkin' about? What is this clan shit all about? I told you I ain't bringing no ashes to Africa for spreading but you insisted—

OHIOGA

(*Interrupting*)

STOP! A performing baboon who tries too hard to outclass his colleagues may expose his anus.

SEGUN

(*Runs to the centre in defense of WYNDEL*)

Gaabaidu! This man is a children; he is not know anyt'ing about Africa. The land is pollute…what can Blackman do to clean?

ATA

(*Gestures to SEGUN to come close to him*)

You have spoken well stranger. You have spoken as an African. If the owner of a calabash calls it a worthless calabash, others will join him to use it to pack rubbish. The *Ifa* priest has seen it that the land needs cleansing. Before we talk further the cleansing must be done.

OHIOGA

(*In a deep or amplified voice different from his normal*)

For the cleansing, you shall provide seven white traditional kola nuts, the tongue of the parrot that does not fly, a pure white she-goat, and the skin of the chameleon that would be black. There is no elephant that complains about the weight of its trunk. Yes, no elephant is burden by the weight of its tusks. These items are not too much for you.

WYNDEL
(*Angrily*)
I'm not providing nothin' for no cleansing. Momma, what you got to say? Ain't this enough foolishness?

AKIN
Hold it Mr. Blackman. Culture is culture anywhere. Before the king we speak with humility. Gaabaidu! Forgive his anger. A piece of iron can only become what the blacksmith says it should become.

UFEDO
(*Has moved to stand next to AKIN, puts her hand on his arm, and speaks as much to him as to the rest of the assembly*)
The words of a young man can be as wise as those of an elder. The man who drives an automobile can know what the priest does not. Who among us does not appreciate such understanding? Even if it comes from one who is not Igala, should we not listen?

ATA
Wife, do not speak out of turn. Do not allow your admiration for the stranger to override the customs of your people.

WYNDEL
Customs, culture? What of them? You folks talk about nuts and about parrots that don't fly and you try to sound like you're making

sense. You don't make any more sense than some of them White men back home. One thing I know is you talk about abominations by cremating my Daddy. What did you want us to do, bring him here all decaying and smelling? What about our culture? I may not know your ways, but one thing I've learned is when people start talking about sin they're mostly talking about what they done wrong themselves.

SEGUN
Shh, Mr. Blackman. You offend the king and you offend the gods of the Igala. Them vex well well. No talk, not offend again, Blackman.

WYNDEL
Well, they offend me. I'm a man, a Black man, a proud Black man and I'm tired of being judged.

ACHIMI
Would you prefer to be hanged from a tree and beaten like the hide of a zebra to soften you? You are new to the ways of your ancestors, but they are the ways of your people before your great-grandfather's father left this place. The king's forbearance is limited. Do not tread too heavily.

UFEDO
Amideju! The man who trains a dog with kindness does not worry about his herd.

OHIOGA
The man who trains his dog must teach that animal to recognize his owner's herd.

MOMMA
Good king—

OHIOGA
Hold your tongue woman. The rat has nothing to say in the gathering
of the cats.

SEGUN
Mr. Blackman provides all everyt'ing. My son, Akin, and me help
him. The land of Igala sacred. T'ings done abomination must be
clean.

ATA
When the priest's instructions have been followed, then we shall
decide what must be done with the Daddy Blackman's ashes. Then
we shall decide who may speak before the King of his people.

BLACK

End of Act One

ACT TWO
Scene 1

WYNDEL paces about in a bedroom within the ATA's palace. The room is well furnished by African standards. The suitcases from act 1, Scene 1 sit to one side of a mirror. The plastic bags of WYNDEL's father's ashes are on the floor beside the bed. WYNDEL's cell-phone and a book are on the bed. The photo of Margarita is on the bookshelves but slightly turned away. WYNDEL comes to a stop in front of the mirror and takes a close look at his reflection.

WYNDEL
(*Absent mindedly*)
What the hell am I doing here? In Africa?
(*Asking his reflection in the mirror*)
What are you doing in a shit hole?
(*There is a knock on the door.*)

(*Loudly*)
Leave me alone Momma.
(*The lock turns and door opens. AKIN and UFEDO enter.*)

AKIN
Not Momma... we are...

WYNDEL
(*Turning to face them*)
Ah, Ufedo! I've been wanting to talk with you. What's that about the king calling you his wife?

AKIN

Are you comfortable in here? The ATA considers you a welcome guest an honored guest...at least for now.

WYNDEL

No, I ain't comfortable. A cage can be furnished beautifully, but it's still a cage. This bird would rather roost on the roofs of Cincinnati if you don't mind. Being held prisoner in a palace isn't my idea of being welcome or honored, not for now or never.

AKIN

As soon as the sacrifice is ready, you will be—

WYNDEL
(*Interrupting*)
Yeah, Akin, what gives with that sacrifice stuff? Seriously, am I supposed to come up with that shit?

AKIN

That is not yours to handle, Mr. Blackman. My father is already working on that. He will go to see the *Ifa* priest first thing in the morning. He will bring him a white she goat and some kola nuts and pay him the money he wants and he will forgive you. Then you can spread your father's ashes and we can leave. My father and I are not welcome here. I don't know about you and your mother, but we have over-stayed.

WYNDEL

As far as I'm concerned, we over-stayed the minute we arrived. But, are you saying the priest is holding us up for money? That Segun just has to pay him...? Wow, what a crock. All that sacrifice stuff doesn't mean nothing?

UFEDO

I fear that Akin does not understand the ways of the Igala, Mr. Blackman. Ohioga has set the price of your sacrifice. How to pay it will become known. You have come home to your people...this is your origin. You must learn the Igala ways. You have reacted badly before my husband the king. He has forgiven you from his kindness, but you must understand—

WYNDEL

(*Interrupting*)

What people are my people? This ain't my home. Come with me to America... to Cincinnati and I'll show you my home, my ways, I'll—

UFEDO

(*Interrupting*)

There is always a root Mr. Blackman. Even as the corkwood tree knows its place, every man should be proud of his origin...his roots.

WYNDEL

(*Angrily*)

Enough talk about this root business. My roots ain't here in Africa and they aren't about some king or some crazy sacrifice.

AKIN

Mr. Blackman, calm down. There is no need for this outburst. Everything is under control.

WYNDEL

(*Still in anger*)

Don't tell me no shit about anger! Momma brought me here to this shit hole. Shit about sacrifices... You want to talk about sacrifices? How about you sacrificing your life, Ufedo? You marrying that king. He's old enough to be your father. What are you doing? I thought you and me...

(*Akin stiffens at this last line. He touches UFEDO who pulls away.*)

You sure have some explaining to do.

UFEDO

Sacrificing my life? What do you mean Mr. Blackman?

AKIN

Wyndel, watch what you say. The antelope that cries out in pain attracts the lion.

UFEDO

What do you want me to explain Mr. Blackman?

WYNDEL

What is the shit about you being the king's wife? His third wife? What's that about

AKIN
Wyndel, this is Africa—

WYNDEL
(*Interrupting*)
You ain't hiding this under the blanket of 'this is Africa'. Let her explain. What the hell kind of shit is that?

UFEDO
Fine! You want an explanation and that you shall have. Have it at the back of your mind that I owe you no explanation, but let me amuse your curiosity. Let me tell you as it is if that will help you to calm your nerves.

AKIN
(*Reaches for UFEDO as he speaks, but she pulls away*)
Ufedo, stop. Let's go. We can talk in the morning. Wyndel needs to rest...we all need rest. We must not say things that should not be said. We ought to go to our rooms and get to sleep.

UFEDO
Not until I am done explaining. Not until Mr. Blackman understands what is right for our people. It is our culture that I marry the king. I am to be his third wife. That is how it should be, and that is how it will be. As the Princess Inikpi was willing to follow the will of the gods and give her life for our people, so, too, I am willing to do what is required.

WYNDEL

What exactly does that mean? What do you mean by culture? What is required?

UFEDO

Yes, culture Mr. Blackman. I was betrothed to the great ATA from my birth. An arrangement done by my father without my consent—

WYNDEL
(*Interrupting*)
Wait! Stop! Without your what?!

AKIN

Mr. Blackman, this arrangement is not new to us. That was how my Mama married my father and there are very happy today.

WYNDEL

Akin, this isn't about you and your daddy. This is about her... about Ufedo. Let her explain the shit she's talking about. I thought...

UFEDO

Yes, it is about me. It is not about what you thought. It is about me. About me and about me alone Mr. Blackman. What more explanation do you seek? I am going to be the ATA's third wife. It is my destiny. What more do you seek?

WYNDEL

Is that what you want? Didn't you say you're educated? Don't you know more of the world? Why do you want totrap your ass in this shithole?

UFEDO
I was on my way home from school, from the University of Lagos
where I have been studying when I met you at Akure. You gave me a
lift, for that was the design of the gods and ancestors. It was my
destiny to lead you to the palace. It may interest you to know that the
king paid my tuition fees. The king and his family have taken
responsibility for me right from my childhood and I am—
(*There is a knock on the door.*)

WYNDEL
Who the hell? What now?

(*The lock turns and door opens. MOMMA enters.*
 WYNDEL continues. He gestures at UFEDO when appropriate)
Momma, you wanted me to come to Africa. Well, damn, I did. Did
you have any idea what we'd find here? Sacrifices and women
married too young. Hell, she was married off at birth. How can—

MOMMA
(*Interrupting*)
Son, we need to talk.

WYNDEL
Go on then, talk, like it'll make sense.

MOMMA
Alone.

WYNDEL

Talk if you want to talk. You can't talk to me alone. This is Africa.
There doesn't seem to be no alone here. Talk in front of them.

AKIN

Mr. Blackman, Wyndel, we can excuse you.

WYNDEL

Stay! Both of you, just stay. Let's talk. Let's talk this out.

AKIN

It is a foolish goat who stays to watch lions argue.
(*He starts towards the door, turns back to gesture to* UFEDO *that she should
exit with him. She goes up to* WYNDEL *as if to shake his hand and passes
him a note.*)

MOMMA

Please Wyndel, you got to listen to me. We have to get this sacrifice
business over with and go back to America as soon as possible before
you do something stupid. I know you. I can see what's brewing inside
you. Segun will pay the priest for us. I talked with him. It won't
cost—

WYNDEL

(*Interrupting*)
Just like that. We just run away. What about roots? What about
meeting the right girl? What about discover—

MOMMA

(*Interrupting*)
No, Wyndel, you don't go getting' up on no high horse. Just listen. We get your Daddy's ashes spread and we get back to Lagos, then back to America, back to Cincinnati, and you back to Margarita.

WYNDEL
Oh, now you want me to be with her? What happened to 'she's not right for you'? What happened to 'find out who you are'? No, Momma, I'm staying until I get to what I need to know or maybe. I'm staying until I get to the root of this.

MOMMA
The root of what Wyndel?

WYNDEL
The root of me. The root of being here. The root!

BLACK

73

ACT TWO
Scene 2

The ATA's audience room. Dominated by one large chair. Present are ACHIMI, OHIOGA, and SEGUN. OHIOGA carries a staff or spear which is the symbol of his office. ACHIMI carries a small whisk like the one the ATA carries but much smaller and made from the tail of an ass rather than a horse.

SEGUN
Why ATA call me? I no do nothing wrong.

ACHIMI
(*Waving his whisk in the manner the ATA has used*)
The ass does nothing wrong but still he is beaten.

OHIOGA
(*Pointing at SEGUN with his spear*)
Achimi, this ass has bourn blasphemers into our midst. He knows why he will be beaten.

ACHIMI
On the other hand, perhaps the king will be merciful. Perhaps he will give you carrots instead of stripes.
(*He swishes the whisk as if it were a whip*)

SEGUN
You go fit... I mean, I beg, if you go speak... My son and I meant no harm. How were we to know that these Americans go spoil your land?

ACHIMI
Has there ever been a time when Americans have not defiled our land? They are almost as bad as the British.

OHIOGA
At least the British went away.

ACHIMI
Leaving a none working nation behind.

OHIOGA
None working? Do you complain that you are in the majority?

ACHIMI
I complain that the land of the Igala is ruled from Lokoja, Abuja and Lagos.

SEGUN
Right now, I wish I was in Lagos.

ACHIMI
(*Using his whisk to stir an imaginary pot*)
Perhaps after he has roasted you in the fire, the ATA will grant your wish and return your ashes to that city of fools and infidels.

SEGUN
I beg of you, what t'ing may I do that soften the king's anger? I will give you what I have if you will speak for me and for Akin.

OHIOGA
(*Pointing his spear at SEGUN*)
And, what will you give me to say that the Americans have fulfilled the sacrifice so they can also leave the Land of the Igala?

SEGUN
I think that na your game. You no want to cleanse land but to chop their money.

OHIOGA
(*Making as if he will actually use the spear to hurt SEGUN*)
Is that the way of the Yoruba priests, to take money instead of honoring their kings and their gods? Is that what you think I, Ohioga, do? Achimi, this Yoruba is a bigger fool than you.

ACHIMI
(*Clutching his heart in mock despair.*)
You wound me, Ohioga. You do me dishonor. If I am not the greatest fool in the land then surely the ATA will send me away. Then I will be forced to wander the streets of Lagos like a taxi driver. Better the honest beatings of a fool than to scurry the streets of the big city looking for a morsel of bread and a cardboard box in which to hide. Does not the lowly rat know he is better in the palace than naked on the streets?

SEGUN
If you not want money, what you want? What you want Segun and Akin do?

OHIOGA

I want the land of my people to be cleansed. I want the sacrifice to be made. When that is done, the Americans may leave and you will be allowed to leave with them. That is the will of the *Ifa*. That is my will as the high priest of the Igala and it is the will of our ATA.

There is nothing more sacred than the land into which your roots sink. Nobody is more worthy of scorn than he who would defile that land. This is the land of the Igala. For years beyond counting we have lived here. For years beyond counting the ATA has ruled his people. When he dies he comes again in his son who honors his father and his father's fathers back to the beginning of our people.

The land has been defiled. It must be cleansed. The gods have spoken. They have named the sacrifice to be made. The king has spoken. He has told the Americans to bring the sacrifice. There is nothing more to be said.

SEGUN

Nothing too much oh! But there is no anyt'ing as a parrot that not fly or a chameleon that turn black. What is the riddle of these t'ings? How do we solve?

OHIOGA

If the gods have demanded them, then this Black Man will find them. The gods do not demand more than a man can do but neither do they make the discovery easy.
(*He bangs the end of his spear on the floor and then exits*)

ACHIMI

What the Black man from America discovers will be what he came here to find. Meanwhile, you and I should lose ourselves in beer.

SEGUN
You go drink beer with a Yoruba man?

ACHIMI
I am no fool; I will drink beer with whoever is willing to pay for it.

BLACK

ACT TWO
Scene 3

WYNDEL's room in the palace. He paces back and forth and reads the note that UFEDO has given him in Act 2, scene 1.

There is a sound at the door. As the door opens

WYNDEL
What took you so long? I've...
(*MOMMA enters*)
Oh, it's you.

MOMMA
Who was you expecting, Boy. No mind telling me otherwise. I know who it is; it's that gal. We got to talk, Wyndel. We got to plan how we is getting out of here. Forget her. She's a good looker and all, but she is trouble—big trouble. You want that ATA fella take and feed you to them lions I heard roaring last night. You want him feeding me to them lions, too? Seriously?! We got to figures out how we is gonna get back to Cincinnati. We get back home and I'll...I'll try to like her.

WYNDEL
Momma, I'm in love. Forget Margarita. I never knew what love is. Every time I see her my heart beats so hard my chest feels like it will fly open. Every time I think of her—

MOMMA
(*interrupting*)

79

Looks more like lust than love to me, but that don't matter. That gal ain't interested in you. She's married to a king. Maybe not the king of no England or nothing big like that, but a real king and you ain't but an assistant manager in a branch of a bank. Do you really think you—

WYNDEL
(*Holding up the note and interrupting*)
She's coming back. See, she gave me this.

MOMMA
(*Taking the note and reading it*)
How do you know that king fella or the priest ain't got somebody watching you? She show up here and both of you are... Lord, have mercy. I wish I was home right this instance.

WYNDEL
Are you saying you made a mistake coming here? Bringing Daddy's ashes back to Africa? Are you saying you shouldn't have dragged me here on this mission of yours? Maybe you just should have left well enough alone, hey Momma. Maybe Margarita would have been enough. But, now, now that I know Ufedo, now that I know what love is, well, I'm glad you did. Mistake or not, I'm glad. Maybe I learned something from you after all. Maybe even mistakes can lead to something good.

MOMMA

I don't know about no mistake. The problem I got right now is you don't got the sense of a gnat. Wanting this gal and that and never thinking 'bout what you is doing. Wyndel, you're a dis—

WYNDEL
(*Interrupting*)
Momma, I've been disappointing you since the day I first drew breathe. Least, that's the way you keep telling it. And every woman I've met has been a disappointment, too. I love Ufedo and I think she loves me. King or no king, I'm tired of doing what other people expect. You are right about the bank. It doesn't mean shit. I don't want to go back to being somebody's house nigger, somebody's Oreo. I may not be from Africa, but I sure as hell—
(*He stops speaking as a noise is heard. The lock of the door turns. Both WYNDEL and MOMMA hold their breath as UFEDO enters.*)

WYNDEL and MOMMA
(*Speaking at the same time*)

WYNDEL
You came. I knew you would.

MOMMA
What you doin' here, girl you want to get my son kilt?

UFEDO
Heart and duty; when they do not agree, which should I follow? I must decide.

81

MOMMA
What you got to do is leave my boy alone.

WYNDEL
No, Momma, what you have to do is leave your son alone. I ain't a boy, not anymore. I'm grown and I'll—

UFEDO
What if the ATA won't let me?

WYNDEL and MOMMA
(*Speaking at the same time*)

MOMMA
Wyndel, you is all I got.

WYNDEL
If I have to, I'll fight for you.

MOMMA
(*Now speaking on her own*)
Who you gonna fight? Him? That king fella? His bodyguard? The whole palace? All the folks here?

WYNDEL
Whoever I need to.
(*To UFEDO*)
I'm not giving you up.

UFEDO
Then we must flee. We must runaway.

MOMMA
Even if you could get away, Wyndel, would you leave me here. Why these savages—

WYNDEL
(*Interrupting*)
A couple weeks ago these people were my ancestors, my roots. Now, you're calling them savages. I don't see anything so savage about them. We broke their laws, but that, Momma, is on you. So far, they've given us a place to sleep, a hell of a lot more comfortable than that crappy hotel in Lagos and some good food. We may have to run. I may have to fight. But, savage is as savage does.

MOMMA
Maybe we should leave this arguing for another time. Ufedo, if you and Wyndel could get out of the palace, could you make it to Lagos before the ATA's guards caught you.

UFEDO
(*Shakes her head*)

MOMMA
And, if you do run away, is there any way I could—

UFEDO

No, Momma Blackman would stay here. Perhaps ATA forgive. Perhaps not. When badger go into bee hive, bees swarm and sting but when badger leave, they forget. When badger go into wasp nest, wasps not forget, they try to kill badger.

WYNDEL
(*To Ufedo*)
I can't leave my mother. Damn, I'd like to, but I can't.

WYNDEL and UFEDO
(*At the same time*)

UFEDO
No, we must not leave her.

WYNDEL
Not saying I wouldn't want to.

MOMMA
Did your Daddy ever tell you how come his great-great-granddaddy were slaved?

WYNDEL
I don't know that talking about ancient history is gonna help.

MOMMA
(*Ignoring her son, talking over him, but still talking to him*)
He was sold by his own folks. That's what he said. Least, that's the why your Daddy had been told. Yes sir, sold by his own people.

WYNDEL
Momma, that was years ago. What does—

UFEDO
(*Putting her hand on his arm or otherwise stopping him and interrupting*)
Sometimes the past gives us the way to the future.

WYNDEL
And sometime it's just old tales that don't make no sense at all.

BLACK

ACT TWO
Scene 4

Evening. AKIN and SEGUN are seated in the courtyard of the ATA's palace. As the lights come up, they are clearly in a heated discussion.

SEGUN
This not one of plays you read for school. You must t'ink about what is real not act fool part.

AKIN
Don't you t'ink I know this, Father. But, when the gods have placed the zebra on the edge of a mountain he has no choice but to become a goat.

SEGUN
And what god done play with your head like this? What god come turn your brain into a mash of cassava?

AKIN
Father, it is not my brain but my heart that the gods have played with.

SEGUN
She is witch who tempted you and the White man who calls self Blackman; he will lead us to disaster.

AKIN

Ufedo is not a witch. She is the perfect woman and you know this for I see you look at her as do all the men in this village.

SEGUN
I see way them look at her and then they look great ATA. When they look his face, they quick quick look away.

AKIN
Well, I cannot. My heart will not—

SEGUN
(*Interrupting*)
You and that White Man, una be two fools, two yeye people.

AKIN
Wyndel's skin may not be the same shade as yours and mine. He may be my rival for Ufedo's love. ... But, Father, he is not a White Man.

SEGUN
Well, he is not Black Man. He is t'inks like he is from England or from America.

AKIN
He is from America.

SEGUN
I no talk of where he raised oh, but where his soul is to be found.

AKIN

So you t'ink Mr. Blackman coming to his father's home—

SEGUN

(*Interrupting*)

Na yeye man job. Achimi is not so great a fool as this White Man.

AKIN

It is not foolish to love.

SEGUN

No, 'e no be foolish to love, but 'e be very foolish to t'ink say your love will reward. The guinea fowl fit yearn for the peacock, but the peacock not notice am? The gnu may follow the giraffe, but he will not see the crocodile waiting in the river. The—

AKIN

(*Interrupting*)

Enough, Father, I understand what you say. Still, the heart does not listen to reason. If Wyndel is a fool for loving Ufedo, am I any wiser.

SEGUN

You be wiser of you listen to father. He here to pull you from the edge of river before the crocodile take you do supper food.

(*UFEDO steps out of the shadow.*)

UFEDO

(*Weeping as she speaks*)

I wish you had said no. I wish that you had left me in the streets of Akure. Better to walk to Kogi. Better to be eaten by hyenas on road.

AKIN and SEGUN
(*At the same time*)

AKIN
Don't worry, Ufedo, I won't let anyt'ing happen. I protect you no matter what ATA say

.

SEGUN
Better I not bring my son to this place. What will happen to him? What will ATA say?

AKIN
Don't worry about me. It is Ufedo whom we must protect.

SEGUN
When the big gorilla see female present her buttocks to another, it is not the female against whom he beats his chest.

UFEDO
Your father is right, Akin. I do not cry for myself but for Wyndel.

AKIN
For Wyndel? The Black man who t'inks like he is White will leave and go back to his Cincin City. Why do you worry about him? It is I who love…

SEGUN and UFEDO
(*At the same time*)

UFEDO
What foolishness is this? I love Wyndel.

SEGUN
Yeye boy. At least he see in heart say Wyndelis White Man.

AKIN
(*To himself. While he is speaking, Ufedo and Segun are both lost in their own thoughts*)
If Wyndel leave, will Ufedo love me? I could steal her from the ATA. I will make sex to her and she will have my son. Then the ATA will not want her. Once she is free, she will know that I provide good life. I will start a troupe of dancers and actors and earn money for her and our children. Maybe, ATA make Wyndel leave. If he t'inkWyndel and Ufedo do t'ings they shouldn't, then ATA will be angry. Once he t'inkWyndel gone, I make sex with Ufedo.

SEGUN
What good is to go to school when brain not t'ink? Akin's brain go asleep, not wake up until he has been dead. I will help the White Blackman. When chimpanzee want steal, he make noise so othersgo look see. Well, well, Blackman make noise and I steal my son from witch.
(*To UFEDO*)
What make king give wife away? You want Wyndel? We must make king give you him.

90

(He takes her by the arm and walks her off stage)

UFEDO
Only the priest can make ATA change his mind.

SEGUN
Then we talk priest, but you promise not go with Akin.

AKIN
(Now alone on the stage)
I will talk to the priest. If he tell ATA that Blackman love Ufedo, ATA will make Blackman go back to America. Then he not want Ufedo as his wife and I can win her.
(He leaves the stage in the opposite direction from that taken by Ufedo and Segun)

Lights dim slowly

ACT TWO

Scene 5

The ATA's throne room. AKIN and OHIOGA are talking. To one side ACHIMI is practicing his juggling and other tricks.

OHIOGA

The fool who thinks he can keep the gourds of life in the air does not appreciate the humor of the gods. You, Yoruba, do you take me for the fool or yourself.

AKIN

I don't t'ink you are a fool, Priest. And, I am soon to graduate university so I—

OHIOGA
(*Interrupting*)
Education is the fastest way to become a fool.

ACHIMI

I have studied my entire life and have learned nothing. But, what should a fool know?

OHIOGA
(*Ignoring the jester*)
Only a fool would come to me with this tale. If the White Man loves Ufedo, then he must die. Any man who loves the wife of the ATA must die. To ask the king to drive him into exile would be sacrilege.

ACHIMI
(*He does a trick making something vanish as he says this*)
To the smart priest everything can be turned into a sacrilege. Confess your sins, make a sacrifice, and the sin goes away. You live to sin again next day. Meanwhile, the priest counts your blessings in his pot.

AKIN
If the ATA killed this man, the Americans might come with bombs and guns. We will all be killed.

ACHIMI
Every man must die no matter whom he loves. To worry about death is to miss the meaning of life. To worry about life is to miss the meaning of death. Since we know nothing of death and much of life, it is pointless to worry about death's meaning. Death and life, who is to say which is better?

OHIOGA
This fool is too wise. A wise fool can become conscience to a king.

ACHIMI
(*Doing a head stand*)
Only if he is fool enough to lose his head.

AKIN
Is there no way to save the White Man's life?

ACHIMI
(*Flipping to his feet*)

93

Only if he by right is the king. That turns everything upside down and makes the past the future.

AKIN
What is he talking about?

OHIOGA
It's an old wives' tale. Nothing of consequence. Many years gone. We cannot see what the river has carried to the ocean.

ACHIMI
What is gone is not always gone. Sometimes the lion you have sent away comes back to bite your ass.

AKIN
This riddle is lost on me.

OHIOGA
When truth is lost it is often better that we not look for it.

ACHIMI
(*Pretending to find a coin of great worth behind the priest's ear*)
Sometimes, it just pops up. I think this Wyndel man has popped.
(*Makes a popping sound*)

OHIOGA
And with him the Igala nation.

AKIN

Will you help me? Will you tell the great king this man wishes to steal his wife?

ACHIMI
Here is a riddle, Akin. How can a man steal what is rightfully his?

AKIN
I do not understand you, Fool.

ACHIMI
That is because fools speak truth while wise men tell lies.

AKIN
Obviously, I waste my time talking these t'ings with you.
(*He leaves*)

ACHIMI
Do you think it possible, Priest? Are the stories true? Was the true king sold to the white men? Did his brother steal the throne? Is this Blackman the descendant of our true ATA?

OHIOGA
You ask many questions but I have not answers. Does he know the names of the ancestors? That will tell us the truth, for the gods require that a man knows from whence he comes. The gods require that a man knows his roots.

BLACK

ACT TWO
Scene six

The throne room the next morning. The ATA is on his throne with ACHIMI at his feet. OHIOGA is seated on a smaller chair nearby. UFEDO stands to one side. SEGUN and AKIN stand next to each other slightly off from directly in front of the ATA. Directly in front of him stands WYNDEL.MOMMA stands behind and to the side of her son. WYNDEL holds the ashes of his father. SEGUN has a small bag. A white she goat is tethered to one side of the stage.

SEGUN
(*Holding the bag in front of him*)
Gaabaidu! You go rein long king. May I speak?

ACHIMI
Speak all you wish, but nobody will hear.

ATA
(*Poking the jester*)
Silence. Everyone be still. Before we can talk, I must know from the priest if the sacrifice has been completed.

OHIOGA
(*Standing and walking to the center of the stage*)
Segun, Wyndel Blackman, have you brought me the necessary items. Have you brought seven white traditional kola nuts, the tongue of the parrot that does not fly, a black she-goat, and the skin of the chameleon that would be black?

96

SEGUN

(*Again holding up the bag*)

Here, Priest, are the kola nuts.

(*He points in the direction of the goat*)

There is the she-goat. … As for the other t'ings, I do not have them. We have searched but we have not found.

WYNDEL

Your highness, I think that I have figured out the Priest's riddle.

(*Turning to his mother*)

Here is the parrot that does not fly. During our stay in your kingdom, she has learned to hold her tongue.

(*Turning back to the ATA and placing his hands on his own breast*)

And here is the chameleon who would be black. All my life I have lived to get by. I have played the parts assigned by those who expected of me. That is why I had come to this kingdom. I did not expect to find myself here. I did not expect to find my roots. Now, I know what it is to be proud of my heritage. My skin may not turn the rich, dark color of the Igala, but in my heart I wish to be as them.

ATA

(*Turning to OHIOGA*)

What do you say, Priest, has he fulfilled the sacrifice?

OHIOGA

Gaabaidu! He has. He has cleansed the land.

ATA

Then permission is given to you. You may bury your father's ashes instead of spreading it and then you and your mother may leave our lands. And you taxi driver, you, too, are free to go. Take your son and leave our lands.

OHIOGA
Gaabaidu! I believe there is yet another matter.

ATA
(*Poking ACHIMI*)
Of what does the priest speak, Fool.

ACHIMI
Master, he speaks of that which makes fools of all men.

UFEDO
(*Steps forward*)
Ohioga will speak of others, my husband, but it is I who am to blame. It is not men but this foolish woman.

ACHIMI
There is no fool greater than the one who asks that the punishment be theirs.

ATA
What punishment? Stop talking in riddles. Priest, what is this topic?

OHIOGA

It is many years since. Many ATAs have ruled and gone to their ancestors. Still the story lives. It is said that Ayegba, the great ATA, had a son, who was named after him and who should have been our ruler after him, but Ayegba's brother was jealous of the throne but even more he was in love with the woman who was to become his nephew's wife. When his nephew was a young man, his uncle made him prisoner during a dark night and sold the boy to men who took slaves. Then he took the boy's clothes, ripped them and dipped them in blood so that the people would believe their prince had been killed by wild beasts.

Because, Ayegba had no other sons, the throne passed to his brother and from him to his son and so the throne has passed until it is now yours oh great ATA.

ATA

I have heard this story. So have all the people. We know that it is not true, for the son of Ayegba has never returned, nor have his sons or his son's sons. If this tale were true, surely the gods would have brought them back to our lands.

ACHIMI

Like the great swans who leave in the summer and return in the colder days, surely the descendants of Ayegba would have returned.

OHIOGA

And, who is to say they have not?

(He turns to Wyndel)

Blackman, do you know the name of that great-great-great-grandfather who came as a slave to America?

WYNDEL
Sure, I do. I still carry it just like my daddy and his daddy before him.
The white men wouldn't let us use it as a name when we were slaves,
but in secret we did. That's why it's our middle names not the up-
front one. We were all called Ayegba. Right, Momma?

MOMMA
(*Nods*)
That's true. Show them your passport, Son.

WYNDEL
(*Pulls out his passport and shows it to UFEDO*)

UFEDO
If this is true, is Wyndel not the rightful ATA?

WYNDEL
Whoa. No way I want to take over the kingship. I just want to bury
my daddy's ashes as you have said and go back to America.

ATA
Then we have no problem.

WYNDEL
Well, maybe a small one. You see, I'm in love with UFEDO and I
want to take her with me.

ATA

WHAT?

WYNDEL
I love—

UFEDO
(*Interrupting*)
Don't I get a word in here?

WYNDEL
Of course, I just… Go ahead.

UFEDO
Seems to me that your majesty owes your relative something. Why not give me to him if he'll give up all claim to your throne.

ATA
You wish to go with him to America?

UFEDO
I wish to go with him wherever he goes. That is the nature of true love, we tie ourselves together or else we tie ourselves in knots.

ACHIMI
Even to this city of Cin? Truly, you are as foolish as I.

AKIN
What about me?

SEGUN
Boy, for somebody with education school, you're pretty foolish, too.
You get taxi cab.Someday you find suitable wife well well. Do you
t'ink your mother would welcome a queen into our home? We are
humble people.

OHIGO
Not so humble, for you are wise. Wise enough to guide Wyndel and
Momma here so that they could fulfill what the gods and our
ancestors willed. You will always be welcome here.

BLACK OUT

Publisher's list

If you have enjoyed *Ashes*consider these other fine books from Mwanaka Media and Publishing:

Cultural Hybridity and Fixity by Andrew Nyongesa
The Water Cycle by Andrew Nyongesa
Tintinnabulation of Literary Theory by Andrew Nyongesa
I Threw a Star in a Wine Glass by Fethi Sassi
South Africa and United Nations Peacekeeping Offensive Operations by Antonio Garcia
Africanization and Americanization Anthology Volume 1, Searching for Interracial, Interstitial, Intersectional and Interstates Meeting Spaces, Africa Vs North America by Tendai R Mwanaka
A Conversation…, A Contact by Tendai Rinos Mwanaka
A Dark Energy by Tendai Rinos Mwanaka
Africa, UK and Ireland: Writing Politics and Knowledge ProductionVol 1 by Tendai R Mwanaka
Best New African Poets 2017 Anthology by Tendai R Mwanaka and Daniel Da Purificacao
Keys in the River: New and Collected Stories by Tendai Rinos Mwanaka
Logbook Written by a Drifter by Tendai Rinos Mwanaka
Mad Bob Republic: Bloodlines, Bile and a Crying Child by Tendai Rinos Mwanaka
How The Twins Grew Up/Makurire Akaita Mapatya by Milutin Djurickovic and Tendai Rinos Mwanaka
Writing Language, Culture and Development, Africa Vs Asia Vol 1 by Tendai R Mwanaka, Wanjohi wa Makokha and Upal Deb
Zimbolicious Poetry Vol 1 by Tendai R Mwanaka and Edward Dzonze

103

Zimbolicious: An Anthology of Zimbabwean Literature and Arts, Vol 3 by Tendai Mwanaka

Under The Steel Yoke by Jabulani Mzinyathi

A Case of Love and Hate by Chenjerai Mhondera

Epochs of Morning Light by Elena Botts

Fly in a Beehive by Thato Tshukudu

Bounding for Light by Richard Mbuthia

White Man Walking byJohn Eppel

A Cat and Mouse Affair by Bruno Shora

Sentiments by Jackson Matimba

Best New African Poets 2018 Anthology by Tendai R Mwanaka and Nsah Mala

Drawing Without Licence by Tendai R Mwanaka

Writing Grandmothers/Escribiendo sobre nuestras raíces:Africa Vs Latin America Vol 2 by Tendai R Mwanaka and Felix Rodriguez

The Scholarship Girl by Abigail George

Words That Matter by Gerry Sikazwe

The Gods Sleep Through It by Wonder Guchu

The Ungendered by Delia Watterson

The Big Noise and Other Noises by Christopher Kudyahakudadirwe

Tiny Human Protection Agency by Megan Landman

Ghetto Symphony by Mandla Mavolwane

Sky for a Foreign Bird by Fethi Sassi

A Portrait of Defiance by Tendai Rinos Mwanaka

When Escape Becomes the only Lover by Tendai R Mwanaka

Where I Belong: moments, mist and song by Smeetha Bhoumik

Soon to be released

Of Bloom Smoke by Abigail George

Denga reshiri yokunze kwenyika by Fethi Sassi

Nationalism: (Mis)Understanding   Donald Trump's Capitalism, Racism, Global Politics, International Trade and Media Wars, Africa Vs North America Vol 2 by Tendai R Mwanaka

Ouafa and Thawra: About a Lover From Tunisia by Arturo Desimone

Thoughts Hunt The Loves/Pfungwa Dzinovhima Vadiwa by Jeton Kelmendi

ويَسهَرُ اللَّيلُ عَلَى شَفَتِي...وَالغَمَام by Fethi Sassi

A Letter to the President by Mbizo Chirasha

Litany of a Foreign Wife by Nnane Ntube

Righteous Indignation by Jabulani Mzinyathi:

Notes From a Modern Chimurenga: Collected Stories by Tendai Rinos Mwanaka

Tom Boy by Megan Landman

My Spiritual Journey: A Study of the Emerald Tablets by Jonathan Thompson

https://facebook.com/MwanakaMediaAndPublishing/